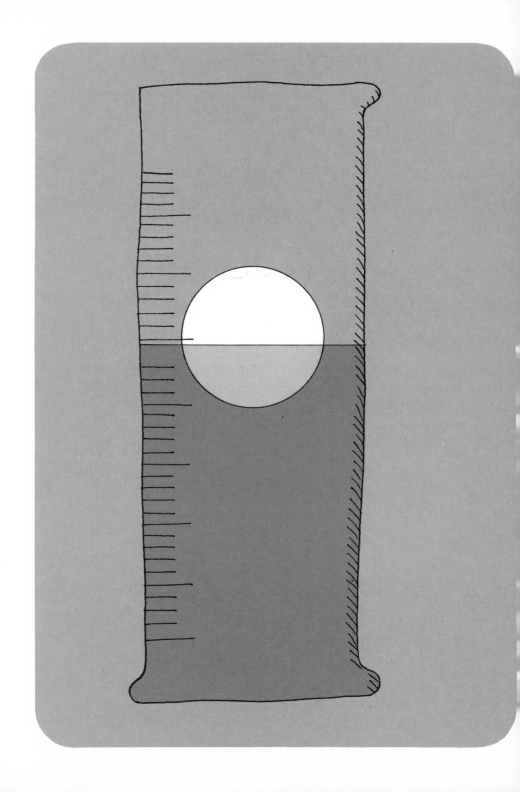

HAVE A BALL

by A. Harris Stone
and Bertram M. Siegel

Illustrated by Peter P. Plasencia

PRENTICE-HALL, INC. • ENGLEWOOD CLIFFS, N.J.

For Bobbi, Bob and Art

530.72
S
cop 1

Have A Ball
by A. Harris Stone and Bertram M. Siegel
© 1969 by A. Harris Stone and Bertram M. Siegel
Illustrations © 1969 by Prentice-Hall, Inc.
Library of Congress Catalog Card Number: 70-76163
Printed in the United States of America • J
13-384180-4
Prentice-Hall International, Inc., London
Prentice-Hall of Australia, Pty. Ltd., Sydney
Prentice-Hall of Canada, Ltd., Toronto
Prentice-Hall of India Private Ltd., New Delhi
Prentice-Hall of Japan, Inc., Tokyo

CONTENTS

INTRODUCTION

Tennis, golf, Ping-Pong, bowling, lacrosse and billiards are all played with balls, so why not buy one ball to play all of these different games? Can you imagine hitting a Ping-Pong ball with a tennis racket and wondering why it doesn't reach the net? Or trying to knock down tenpins with a golf ball?

What makes a Ping-Pong ball act differently from a golf ball? Or a tennis ball differently from a billiard ball? Certainly there are differences in size and color, and some balls are even different in shape. But no one who picked up a golf ball painted to look like a Ping-Pong ball would be fooled by what it appeared to be.

Scientists are, after all, just people. Their curiosity becomes aroused. But scientists, unlike most people, follow up their curiosity by doing experiments. A golf ball's "slice" or a baseball's "curve" might excite a scientist's curiosity and lead him to study the behavior of balls.

If a scientist wanted to find out about balls, he would observe them carefully, do tests on them, and would soon be able to describe each ball as having very different characteristics. During his study of balls, the scientist might discover many properties of matter. This book deals with properties of matter that can be discovered by experimenting with balls. All you need to do is be willing to experiment and HAVE A BALL!

BOUNCEABILITY

Which card is hit when a golf ball is pushed off the shelf? Will the same card be hit if a tennis ball is used instead of a golf ball? How about a Ping-Pong ball?

Will the same card be hit each time the golf ball is dropped from the same shelf? What happens when the same ball is thrown onto the floor from shelf height, instead of being pushed off the shelf?

Tennis, golf and Ping-Pong balls all can bounce. The bounceability of a ball is determined by many factors, including size and weight.

The bounceability of a ball is also determined by its *elasticity*. Some substances may be changed in shape when a force is applied to it. An elastic substance is one that will change and then return to its original shape when the force acting on it is released. How fast the substance returns to its original shape is important. Which ball has the most bounceability—a golf ball, a tennis ball, a Ping-Pong ball or a steel ball? Which has the least?

Do all balls bounce?

How high does a beach ball bounce when it is filled with water instead of air?

DEFORMATION

What is observed on a beach ball that has been bounced on a floor covered with chalk dust? What effect does a harder bounce have on what is observed?

Does the same effect occur when a ball half as large is used? Twice as large?

What happens to the *diameter* of a 2 inch clay ball when it is dropped from a height of 2 feet? Does the same effect occur when the ball is dropped from 4 feet? 6 feet? Does the diameter of the ball before it is dropped have any effect on what occurs? Try clay balls with diameters of 3, 4 and 5 inches.

FORCE

From what height must a baseball be dropped so that it will tear through a piece of waxed paper that has been tightly stretched over a frame?

Does doubling the distance that the ball falls double the number of waxed paper sheets it can tear? Do other kinds of paper tear when the ball is dropped from the same height?

Can a golf ball dropped from the same height as the baseball tear the same number of sheets of paper? How about a ball of clay made to the same size as the baseball? A ball of clay the same size as a golf ball? Which has the greatest effect on the number of sheets of paper that can be torn—the height from which the ball is dropped or the weight of the ball? Does a ball appear to become heavier when it falls a greater distance?

Does it make any difference if there are spaces between the sheets of paper? Try sheets of waxed paper 1 inch apart; 2 inches apart.

MORE FORCE

Can a golf ball be thrown hard enough to shatter a wood board ½ inch thick? How about a tennis ball? A baseball? What is the relationship between the *force* which a ball can exert and the *mass* of the ball? *Caution! Watch out for flying golf balls.*

Could a Ping-Pong ball be thrown, or fired from a popgun, fast enough to break a piece of Saran Wrap stretched across a frame?

What material can be broken by a fast-moving Ping-Pong ball? Does the distance that the ball is thrown have any effect?

The force that a moving ball can exert on a surface is the product of two factors. These factors are the *mass* of the ball and its *velocity*.

People often diet, they say, to lose weight. What they are really trying to do is decrease their *mass*. The mass of an object is often defined as the amount of quantity of "stuff" it contains. The mass of an object on earth can be determined by weighing it. Does the mass of an astronaut change when he becomes weightless?

Why does a fast ball often hurt a catcher's hand when a curve, or change-of-pace ball, thrown by the same pitcher, does not?

Which can exert more force on a catcher's hand—a baseball with a mass of 5 ounces moving with a velocity of 70 miles per hour or a softball with a mass of 7 ounces moving with a velocity of 50 miles per hour?

PLAYING THE ANGLES

A rubber ball can be launched from the device shown below. At what height on the wall does the ball hit if it is launched three feet from the ground?

Coating the ball with chalk dust is helpful in determining how high the ball strikes on the wall.

Does the same effect occur when a golf ball is launched instead of a rubber ball?

The height on the wall that a ball launched from a mailing tube gun reaches is an effect of the angle at which the tube is held. Does the angle at which the tube is held have any other effects? What is the angle between the ball's path and the ground when the tube is held at any angle?

Does the distance between the wall and the spot where the ball strikes the ground change when the tube is held in different positions?

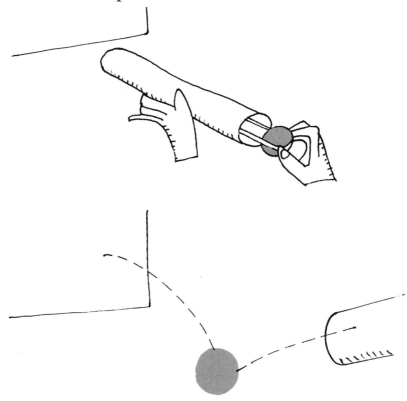

What is the relation between the distance from the wall that the ball hits and the angle that the ball travels?

SPINNING AND ROLLING

How can a beach ball be made to spin while it rolls? Rolling and spinning a ball on a sand-sprinkled floor may be helpful in seeing what path the ball follows.

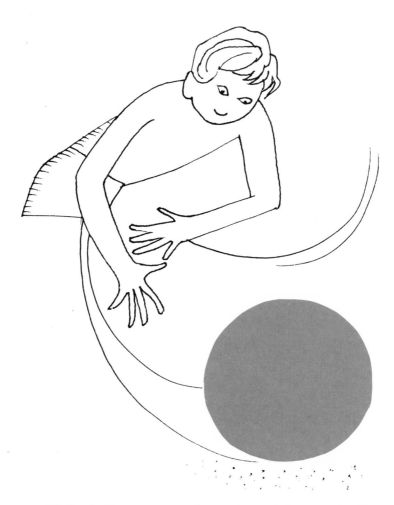

If the ball is spun to the right and bounced off a wall, does it rebound to the right?

Does a baseball really curve? People have argued about this question for many years. Finally, research was conducted to prove that it is possible for a pitcher to make a ball curve. This research showed that a ball can be made to bend as much as 17 inches from a straight line drawn between home plate and the pitcher's mound! The ball that curved 17 inches had a velocity of almost 100 feet per second or 90 miles an hour.

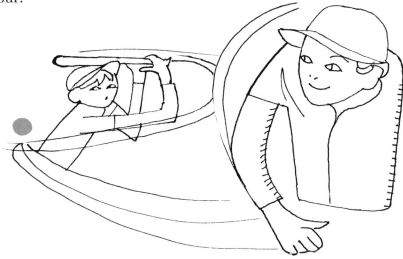

A pitcher makes the ball curve by twisting his wrist quickly as the ball is released. The ball leaves the side of his index finger and thumb. It is sent spinning by this twist of his wrist and by the friction of the pitcher's fingers on the ball's seams. As the ball spins on its axis and moves toward the batter, air moves past the ball faster on one side than it does on the other. This difference in speed causes a difference in air pressure and the ball is pushed toward the area of lower pressure.

Why does a curve thrown by a left-handed pitcher act differently than the same pitch thrown by a right-hander? How can a thrown ball be made to rise or dip?

"ENGLISH"

Can a golf ball be made to stop rolling when, after being struck by the tip of a dowel, it hits a second golf ball? Does striking the dowel near the top of the golf ball have any effect? How about striking it near the bottom of the ball? In the middle?

How can a golf ball be struck with the tip of a dowel so that it will hit a second ball and roll to the left? To the right?

The game of billiards is played with a white ball and 15 numbered balls. The white ball is struck with the tip of a stick so that it will hit a numbered ball and the sides of the table. In pocket billiards, the white ball must cause a numbered ball to roll into a pocket without having the white ball roll in.

How can ball (1) be struck so that it causes ball (3) to roll into pocket A without hitting ball (2)?

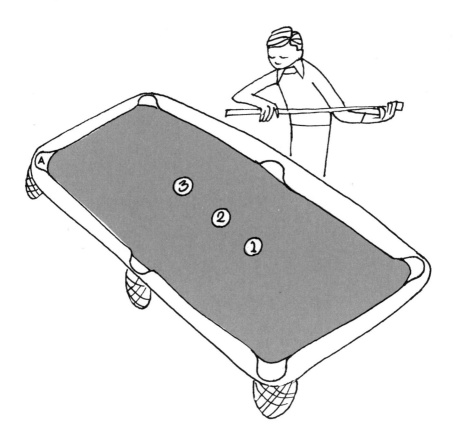

THE LEANING TOWER

Does a softball reach the ground before a baseball when they are both dropped at the same time? Ask an adult and a friend with a tape measure and stopwatch to help with this one. Watch out for pedestrians.

How far does the baseball fall in one second? Try 16 feet. Does it take 2 seconds to fall 32 feet? Three seconds to fall 48 feet? Does throwing the ball downward make any difference in the time it takes to fall?

A falling object travels a distance of 16 feet in its first second of fall but it does not fall 16 feet every second! As an object falls, its velocity does not remain the same. What causes a falling object to *accelerate?*

The graph below shows the data that was collected for an object that fell for 6 seconds. How far did it fall in two seconds? Four seconds? Seven seconds? Does the weight of the object have any effect on the distance it will fall in a given amount of time?

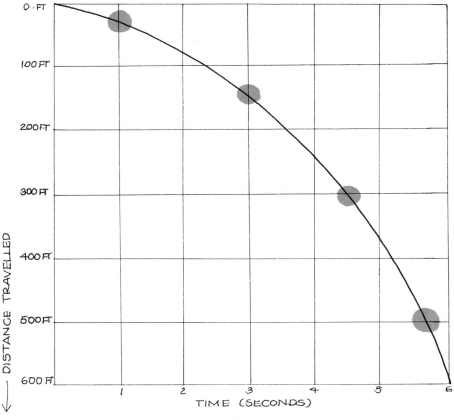

ABOVE AND BELOW

Does the size of a ball have an effect on how much of it floats above water? Try two hollow balls of different sizes but with the same weight. Balls can be made to weigh the same by taping pennies or paper clips to them.

How does the amount of ball above the water line compare to the diameter of the ball? Does the same relationship occur when solid balls of equal weight but different sizes are used?

An iceberg floats with approximately 80 percent of its mass below the water. A balloon floats with almost all of its mass above water. What are the factors that determine how much of a floating object will be above or below water? Does the kind of water have an effect? Try floating two hollow balls in water that has salt added to it. Does the concentration of salt make a difference?

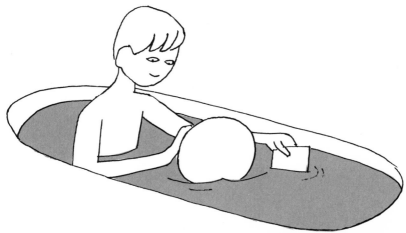

The ideas explaining how and why an object floats were studied in great detail by Archimedes almost 2,000 years ago. It is said that he discovered these principles while trying to solve a problem given to him by the King of Syracuse. The King wanted to know if a crown made for him was of solid gold or if other materials had been mixed with the gold. Archimedes compared the volume of water that was *displaced* by a piece of pure gold equal in weight to the crown, to the amount of water displaced by the crown. He found that each displaced a different volume of water and concluded that the crown was a fraud! Was Archimedes right? Try the crown experiment using some other metals if you can't find enough gold.

PENETRABILITY

What can be seen when equal-sized balls of wood, steel and glass are allowed to stand on a flattened piece of "Silly Putty" for 10 minutes? 30 minutes? Overnight? Does the thickness of the "Silly Putty" have any effect on what occurs?

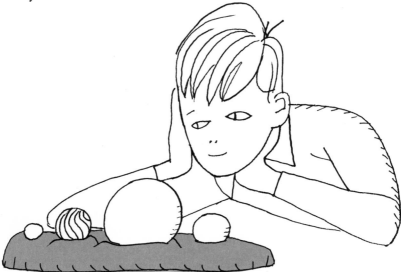

Does the weight of each ball have any effect on what occurs? Would the same effect be seen if balls of various substances but of equal size and weight were used? How about balls of equal weight but with different sizes? Is the same effect seen when the "Silly Putty" and the steel, wooden and glass balls are placed in a refrigerator?

26

The penetrating ability of a ball depends on many factors. These factors include the substance that the ball is made of, the weight of the ball, and the substance into which the ball is penetrating.

Try the balls of wood, steel and glass on a piece of ice. Does the ball that penetrated best into "Silly Putty" penetrate best into ice? List the balls in order of best to poorest penetrator.

Will the same order of best penetrator be produced if wooden, glass and steel balls of equal weight are used?

KNOCKING AROUND

How far will a Ping-Pong ball roll when a golf ball is rolled into it? Does any ball roll the same distance when another ball is rolled into it? Try rolling a golf ball into a tennis ball; a Ping-Pong ball into a golf ball; a baseball into a tennis ball; and a basketball into a golf ball. Which combination of balls results in the longest roll?

Does the speed of the rolling ball have any effect on the distance that the stationary ball moves? Does spinning the ball as it rolls have any effect on what occurs? Does the distance that the ball rolls before it collides make any difference? What happens to the ball that is rolled after it collides with the second ball?

Before an object can be made to move, a force must be applied to it. This force gives the object the *energy* required for motion. A rolling ball can apply a force to another ball and *transfer* to that ball some of its own energy. Where does a rolling ball get its energy? Do all balls require the same amount of energy to make them move? What happens to the energy of a rolling ball when it collides with another ball and the second ball does not move? What happens to the energy of a rolling ball as it slows down and stops? Would a ball roll forever if there were nothing in its way? Why does it take more energy to start an object moving than it does to keep it moving?

What happens to a marble that has been placed on a sheet of tightly stretched plastic when another marble is dropped onto the plastic? Does the distance that the dropped marble falls have any effect on what occurs? Does doubling the distance of fall double the effect?

SQUASHABILITY

How many turns of a vise are required to squash a tennis ball a half an inch? Can the same number of turns be made so that a golf ball is squashed the same amount? How about a Ping-Pong ball?

Can all hollow balls be squashed the same amount by the same number of vise turns? What is inside a hollow ball?

Which is most "squashable"—a golf ball, a solid, hard rubber ball, a "Superball" or a solid steel ball? Which is most elastic? Which bounces highest when dropped from equal heights?

What is the relationship between "bounceability," "squashability," "deformation" and the height to which a ball bounces?

SPINABILITY

What happens to a football that has been set spinning while lying on its side? Does spinning it faster have any effect on what happens?

Will the same effect occur if the football is set spinning on its "nose" and allowed to fall on its side while spinning?

What is the relationship between the general ways in which footballs act and the spin of a football? Can a football be thrown so that it does not spin? What is the relationship between the amount of spin of a thrown football and the distance the ball travels? A football's spin may be easily observed if a piece of white tape is applied to the ball from end to end. Does throwing "underhand" produce as much spin as throwing "overhand"? Which produces a longer throw—underhand or overhand?

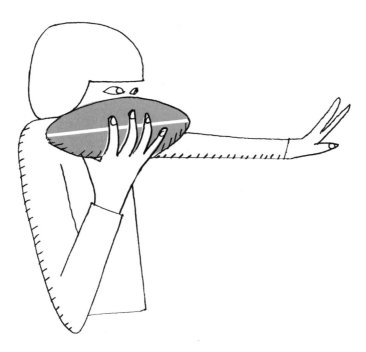

THE LONG AND SHORT OF IT

What happens to the heavy ball when a lighter ball in the apparatus shown below is spun rapidly?

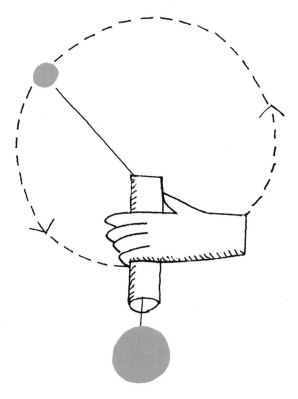

What effect does slowly pulling down on the heavy ball have on the velocity of the light ball? How can the light ball be made to slow down?

Astronomers often describe the earth and moon as being connected to each other. The moon spins around the earth as the earth rotates on its *axis*. This earth-moon system moves through space as the earth revolves around the sun. What would be the effect on the velocity of the moon if it were moved closer to the earth? Would a year be longer if the earth were closer to the sun? Shorter? Still 365¼ days? Would a 12-year-old be 12 if he lived on Jupiter?

Try two balls of equal weight in the experiment described on the previous page. Does the weight of the ball have any effect on how fast it spins?

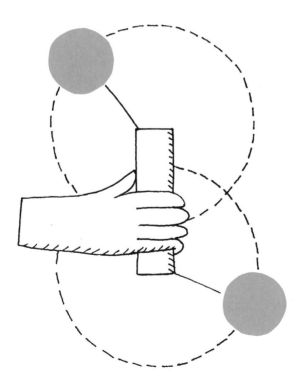

A MARBLE HIGHWAY

How much is an inflated balloon squashed when it is placed between a hand and a heavy block and the hand pushes until the block moves? Try this experiment again with marbles under the block.

Does the number of marbles used under the block have any effect on how much the balloon is squashed? How much is the balloon squashed when rollers are used under the block instead of marbles?

Roads and highways are not made of marbles—or are they? The use of logs and rollers was perhaps the first step in moving large, heavy objects across the ground. Even the Pharaohs, when building the pyramids, relied on rollers to move the massive stone blocks they used. But rollers are inconvenient because someone has to keep moving the rollers from behind the block to in front of it. This problem was partly solved when men started using wheels mounted on axles and carrying the heavy loads on top of the axles. This procedure also had drawbacks. With large weights on axles, the amount of friction in the hub of the wheel became very great and continually wore out both wheels and axles. The friction–wearing difficulty was not solved until some ingenious man decided to line the hub of the wheel with small rollers on which the axle and wheel could turn.

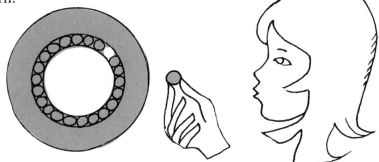

The rollers in the hub of a wheel act to reduce friction and allow the wheels to move more easily. These clever friction reducers are used in almost every wheel today and are called *bearings*. And so even if roads are not made of marbles, marbles have a great deal to do with the wheels that travel over these roads.

Why are bearings in wheels usually packed in grease or bathed in oil? How could a car be made to stop if highways were made out of marbles or bearings?

GOING THROUGH CHANNELS

Will a marble that is allowed to roll freely in a channel reach the same height on the opposite side as it started from? Does it reach its original height when it rolls back?

What forces are acting on the ball to cause it to react the way it does?

In most experiments where objects move, there are a large number of factors which affect what happens. Some of these factors are easily discovered. Some may be difficult to discover because they have only a small effect and therefore are not easily measured. When scientists attempt to discover the forces and factors acting within an experiment, they usually test as many different ideas as they can think of. Even if an idea seems ridiculous, they may test it anyway just to see if it really is ridiculous. To find out what factors are affecting the marble in the trough, experiment with these ideas:

weight of the ball
size of the ball
friction
material of the ball and channel
surface texture of the ball and channel
lubrication
shape of the channel
angle of the channel

TRAJECTORIES

Which marble hits the ground first—one marble dropped from a height of 5 feet or one that is shot horizontal to the ground at a height of 5 feet? The apparatus shown below is helpful in answering this question.

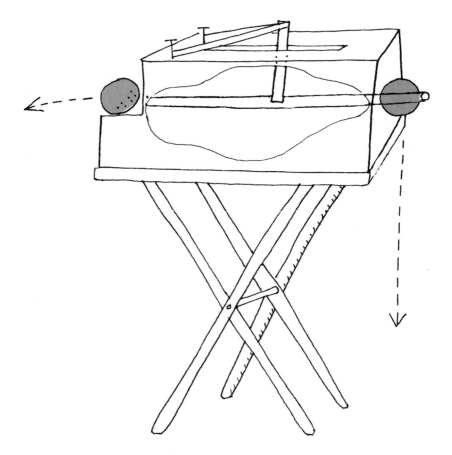

Does it matter if balls of different weights are used? How about size?

Can an object do two things at the same time? Can a ball move *horizontally* while it is moving *vertically?* The path of a ball in flight or of cereal shot from guns is called the *trajectory* of the object. This trajectory usually has two distinctly different parts. One is called its vertical component, the other its horizontal component. Both are usually measured as *acceleration.* What would seem to be the most logical factor affecting the vertical, or up-and-down path of an object's trajectory?

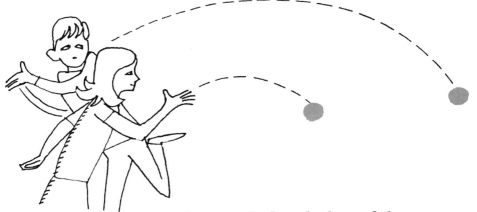

Trajectories are mostly controlled and changed by changes in horizontal acceleration. Which would have the longest trajectory—a baseball thrown as fast as possible or a bullet shot from a gun? Is the trajectory of a bullet fired from a pistol the same as a bullet fired from a rifle? The best experiment to do in order to answer this question is a mental one!

The combination of the vertical and horizontal components of a trajectory are never separated except when the trajectory is being studied. When one component is changed, the other is changed. What are the trajectories of two baseballs, one thrown 50 feet and the other 150 feet? How does the acceleration of these two balls affect their trajectories?

WHAT GOES UP . . .

Does a ball that is thrown straight up come straight down? What happens to a ball that is thrown into the air from a moving object?

Will a heavier ball have any effect on what occurs? Does walking faster make any difference in the way the ball falls?

Forward motion is not the only factor that controls the pathway of a ball that is thrown straight up or one that is dropped straight down. Can a ball be dropped straight down through a tube so that it will bounce straight back into the tube?

Is the path of the bouncing ball different when a fuzzy tennis ball is used instead of a smooth rubber ball?

A SWINGING THING

What is seen when three different balls are set in motion as shown in the illustration below? Try a rubber ball, a tennis ball and a Styrofoam plastic ball.

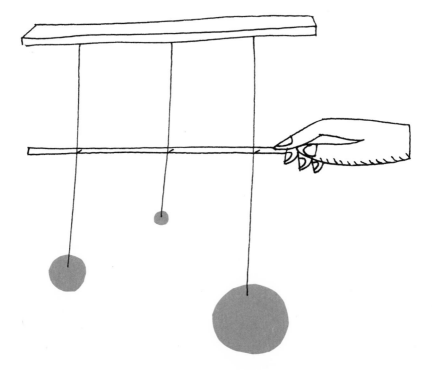

Does the length of the string have any effect on what occurs? Should the three balls be supported by strings of equal length?

Simple physical phenomena can often be adapted to gain information about the characteristics of other phenomena. Sometimes the unique application of an effect can give more detailed information than is otherwise obtainable. What differences can be observed if a steel ball on a string is used as a pendulum in a tank of water? of oil? of molasses? What information can be found about the viscosity of each liquid?

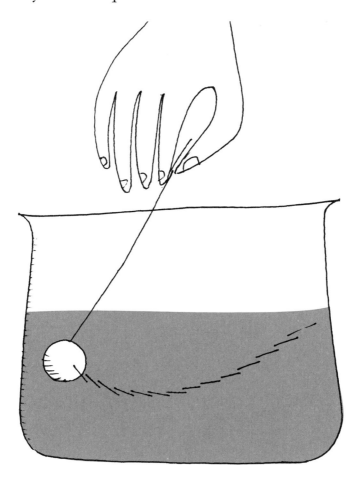

ROQUET

What happens to a line of croquet balls when a ball held tightly under foot is hit into them? Will the same effect be seen if the ball which is hit is not held by foot?

Try striking the ball harder. Does force make any difference in what occurs? Does the distance that the hit ball has to roll have any effect on what is seen?

How much energy is transferred from one ball to another when two balls of equal size and material collide? Does the velocity of one ball affect the velocity of the other? How do two balls moving one behind the other transmit their energy to a line of balls as shown below?

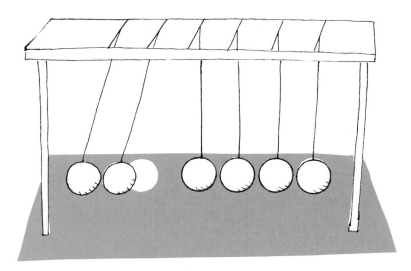

Will a line of balls, where every other one is a different material, react the same way as a line of similar balls? Try baseballs and tennis balls or baseballs and Styrofoam balls.

PACKING

What happens when a jar of BBs is poured into a jar that is "full" of marbles? Which jar can hold more BBs— a quart jar full of marbles or a quart jar full of Ping-Pong balls?

How much water can be poured into a quart jar full of BBs? Can the same amount of water be poured into a quart jar full of marbles?

How much water can be absorbed by a concrete block? a steel block? a brick? The amount of H_2O that can penetrate any of these blocks is determined by the arrangement of the particles that make up the block. If this statement is correct, the reverse of it can be used to determine the relative closeness of particles in a substance. For example, if substance X can absorb 10 times the amount of H_2O than substance Y can absorb, then it is reasonable to think that the particles of substance Y may be 10 times closer together than the particles of substance X.

Which of the following substances have their particles closest together? Farthest apart? Sand; loam; clay; gravel. In what way does the size of particles affect their arrangement? Are particles of the same material the same size?

LOOP-THE-LOOP

Will balls that are propelled down a section of cut hose make a complete "trip" down the hose? What happens when a lighter ball is used?

Is there a speed with which the ball can only reach point A? What is the path of the ball that reaches A and does not continue along the hose?

Some characteristics of an object change when the velocity of the object is varied. One of the characteristics of a ball that is affected by its velocity is its path. So, if a ball's velocity continues to change it is reasonable to believe that its path will also change. Is it true that a ball that is thrown straight up stops before it comes down? If it did not stop going up, would it ever come down? What is the velocity of a bullet when it hits the ground after having been shot straight up? Gabby Street, a baseball player, once caught a baseball thrown from the top of the Washington Monument which is over 500 feet high. How fast was the baseball traveling when he caught it at ground level?

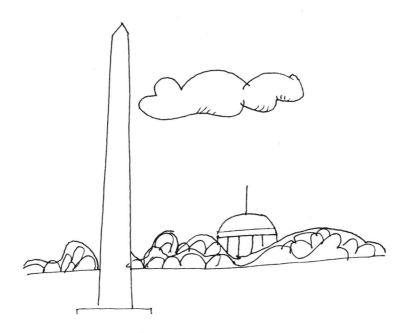

HALF A BALL

What is the difference between the flight patterns of a rubber ball and half of a rubber ball when each has been hit by a bat? Do both travel the same distance?

What is the relationship between how far a half ball travels and on which side of the half ball the bat hits it? Is a half ball deformed more or less than a whole ball when it is hit by a bat?

Kids who live in large crowded cities are often the most ingenious inventors of ball games. Since space for playing is often limited, they sometimes find it very difficult to find an area large enough to play baseball. They use their imaginations and design ball games that can be played where space is not the only limitation. What kind of ball game can be played on a narrow street where buildings full of glass windows always hamper the long ball hitters? In games where a ball is hit, city kids frequently use half balls to limit both distance and damage. And what does a slugger without a half ball do? Try hitting a 3-inch-long section of garden hose with an old broom stick and you will see what a sharp eye a "hoseball" hitter has to have. Can a "hoseball" be hit as far as half a rubber ball? If all the kids shouted, "No divies on the windows!" when you were up at bat, which would you rather hit—a "hoseball" or a half a rubber ball?

A STRANGE BALL

What happens to the shape of a ball made of "Silly Putty" when it is bounced a number of times? Does a hollow "Silly Putty" ball bounce as well as a solid "Silly Putty" ball? Try making a ball with "Silly Putty" around a Ping-Pong ball.

Does a solid "Silly Putty" ball that is thrown at an angle act the same as a rubber ball thrown at the same angle?

Elasticity is the word used to describe materials that usually return to their original shape after being deformed. The substance of which "Silly Putty" is made behaves in a most peculiar way, which may explain the name that is given to it. "Silly Putty" seems to violate all the laws of elasticity. What happens to a ball of "Silly Putty" that is left in a dish overnight? What happens if a wad of it is slowly stretched? If it is rapidly stretched? What happens to a "Silly Putty" ball that is struck sharply with a hammer? What is the relationship between the amount of flattening of a "Silly Putty" ball and the height from which it is dropped?

A STRANGER BALL

Is it possible to bounce a tennis ball hard enough to go over a house? Can a "Superball" be bounced over a house? Get a friend to help with this one or you may lose your ball.

Does the angle at which the ball is thrown affect the height to which it will bounce?

When two balls of equal size and weight are thrown with an equal amount of force and one bounces higher than the other, is it logical to think that the one that bounces higher has more energy? The apparatus shown below can be used to find out by determining how far the cart is moved by each ball that is bounced against it.

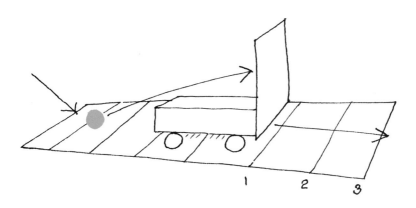

How does using a "Superball" in the other experiments in this book affect the results?

TO BOUNCE OFF YOUR BRAIN

Why does a golf ball have dimples?
Why does a tennis ball have fuzz ?
Why are there holes in a Whiffle ball?
Would a Whiffle ball whiffle if it didn't have holes?

Why isn't a bowling ball inflated rather than being solid?

What makes a new tennis ball sometimes act as if it were "dead"?

Why are tennis balls stored in pressurized cans?

Why is a football kicked with the toe on kick-offs and the instep on punts?

Can you play Ping-Pong with a ball that has 10 or 12 pin holes in it?

Why isn't croquet played with a rubber ball?

Why is jai-alai (hi-li) played with a curved paddle-like glove instead of a flat one?

The hammer thrower and discus thrower in track events are allowed to spin to gain momentum. Why can't the shot putter?

Why are the cushions on a billiard table made of hard rubber rather than steel or wood?

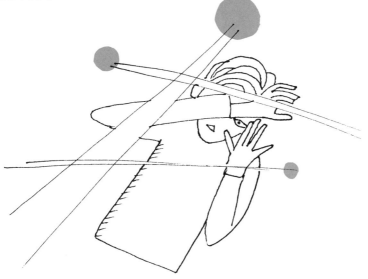

Why is ice hockey played with a puck when field hockey is played with a ball?

Why does a baseball pitcher stand on a mound that is higher than the rest of the field?

GLOSSARY

ACCELERATION—Acceleration is defined as the rate of increase in velocity with respect to time. An acceleration rate of 0 to 60 m.p.h. in 10 seconds may be good for a family car but not for a racer.

ANGLE—The figure formed by two straight lines or rays drawn from a point is called an angle. The space between these rays is also an angle.

BALL—Any round or egg-shaped object used in various games is called a ball. A ball is also a formal social dance.

BASEBALL—Baseball is a game played with a ball and bat by two opposing teams on a field with four bases forming a diamond. A baseball is made with a cork center, layers of rubber and yarn and a horsehide cover.

BILLIARDS—The game of billiards is played with hard balls driven by a cue on a table with raised cushioned edges.

BOWLING—Bowling is a game in which a heavy ball is rolled along a wooden lane aimed at ten wooden pins. Though its surface is made of hard rubber, the inside of a bowling ball is a mixture of rubber and cork.

COMPONENT—In chemistry, a component is one of the ingredients in a chemical compound or mixture. A component is a piece of a whole. As an example, speakers are one component of a high fidelity system.

DIAMETER—The diameter of a circle or sphere is a straight line passing through the center of that figure. The diameter of a circle divides the circle into two semicircles.

ELASTIC—An elastic object is one that can return to its original shape and size after being squeezed, stretched or deformed in some way.

ENERGY—Energy is the ability to do work. Sound, heat, light and electricity are forms of energy.

ENGLISH—A spinning motion given to a ball is often called English. English is also the language spoken in most parts of England and occasionally in the United States.

ENTROPY—Entropy is a measure of the unavailability of energy in a heat energy system. Entropy increases as the available energy decreases.

FOOTBALL—Football is a field game played with an inflated leather ball by two teams. A regulation football weighs about 14½ ounces and is less than 12 inches long. The shape of a football is that of a prolate spheroid.

FORCE—Any influence on an object that, when unopposed, causes the object to move, change speed or change direction, is described as a force. A force may also be described as a push or a pull.

GRAVITY—That force that attracts all objects toward the center of a spinning body, such as earth, is called gravity.

HORIZONTAL—A horizontal line is a line drawn parallel to the plane of the horizon.

HOSEBALL—Hoseball is a game played by any number of players in any available space. The object of the game is to hit a piece of garden hose (thrown by a member of the opposing team) with a broom stick, and to avoid breaking windows.

MASS—Mass is defined as the amount of matter in an object. Mass may be measured in ounces, pounds, grams or kilograms. As an example, the weight of an object may be different if measured on different planets, but the object's mass is the same everywhere.

PENDULUM—A pendulum is a body suspended from a fixed point so that it is able to swing back and forth by the interaction of gravity and momentum.

RATIO—Ratio is a relationship between two numbers or quantities. The ratio of 12 to 6 may be expressed as 12:6 or 12/6 and is equal to 2/1 or 2.

RIGID—A rigid object is inflexible, stiff and unbending. So is a rigid person. A scientist cannot afford to have a rigid attitude toward the results of experiments.

ROQUET—In the game of croquet, to roquet is to hit another player's ball.

TRAJECTORY—The path of a moving object is the trajectory of that object. The trajectory of a bullet fired from a gun has a parabolic shape.

VELOCITY—The speed and direction of a moving object is the velocity of that object. If the velocity changes, the object accelerates.

VERTICAL—A vertical line is upright or straight up and down. A vertical line bisects a horizontal line at an angle of 90 degrees.